FRED FLINTSTONE'S ADVENTURES with LEVERS

Lift That Load!

by Mark Weakland

illustrated by Christian Cornia

Curious Fox
a capstone company-publishers for children

2

3

4

A shovel is a lever that people use to move rocks and soil.

A crowbar is a common lever.
It can be used to loosen nails in
floorboards, for example.

A broom is a lever that makes cleaning work easier.

I bet he could, Fred!

10

The handle of that razor is a lever too. And the pterosaur is just like a pair of scissors. It has two levers - its feet and its beak. Hey, not too much off the top, buddy!

Scissors are a type of lever. The handles and blades attach in the middle at the fulcrum.

14

On a fishing rod, the effort is between the fulcrum and the load.

16

A bottle opener is a lever. Force lifts the load, which is the bottle top.

You really do love levers, Fred.

Look at that, Wilma. Pebbles and Bamm-Bamm are little lever experts. Their catapult is a type of lever. It has a fulcrum, an input force and a load. When Bamm-Bamm applies a force, he can send a load flying!

In a kitchen, levers are used for dishing up food and for eating.

It's good to see you using levers, Wilma. Knives are a type of lever. So are salad tongs. The tongs are two levers joined at an end fulcrum. Spoons and forks are also levers. Don't you just love simple machines, honey?

Sure, Fred.

Glossary

catapult   device that uses a lever to fling objects

effort   force you apply to a lever to move an object

exert   use force to do work

force   push or pull exerted upon an object

fulcrum   resting point at which a lever bar turns

input force   initial force used to get a machine working

load   object that moves when a force is applied

output force   (also called the load) weight of the object to be moved

pivot   point at which something turns or balances

pry   remove, raise or pull apart with force, as with a lever

Read more

How Things Work (See Inside), Conrad Mason
(Usborne Publishing Ltd, 2009)

How Things Work Encyclopedia (First Reference), Dorling
Kindersley (DK Children, 2012)

Making Machines with Levers (Simple Machine Projects),
Chris Oxlade (Raintree, 2015)

Website

www.dkfindout.com/uk/science/simple-machines/
Find out more about how we use simple machines.